‘IF I WERE GO SAY SORRY’

Robert Kirkwood

Lecturer in Religious and Moral Education
Moray House, Edinburgh

Illustrated by

Edward McLachlan

Hodder & Stoughton

A MEMBER OF THE HODDER HEADLINE GROUP

ACKNOWLEDGEMENTS

The publishers would like to thank the following for permission to reproduce copyright material in this volume:
HarperCollins for extracts from *The Great Divorce*, C.S. Lewis; Cambridge University Press for extracts from *The Brothers Karamazov*, Fyodor Dostoevsky.

The publishers would also like to thank the following for permission to reproduce photographs in this volume:
Topham pp14 (both), 34, 46; Riccardo Lupo for the photograph by Mario Lupo p23; Dagnino/Cosmos/ Impact p30 (right); Hulton Deutsch p30 (left).

Every effort has been made to trace and acknowledge ownership of copyright. The publishers will be glad to make suitable arrangements with any copyright holders whom it has not been able to contact.

A Note to Teachers
While God is referred to as 'he' throughout this book, pupils should be made aware that God may be considered to be both male and female.

ISBN 0 340 627433

First published 1995
Impression Number 10 9 8 7 6 5 4 3 2 1
Year 1998 1997 1996 1995

Printed in Great Britain for Hodder & Stoughton Educational, a division of Hodder Headline Plc, 338 Euston Road, London NW1 3BH by Cambus Litho, East Kilbride, Scotland.

CONTENTS

To Ivana

IF I WERE GOD I'D SAY SORRY

1 If God exists, do you think he should say sorry for some of the things he has made? Give reasons for your answer.

I BLAME GOD

Well I'm confused because if God is the creator of the universe then he must have made everything that exists within it. So surely we shouldn't just say he made **'All things bright and beautiful'.** If he is the only creator then he must also be responsible for **'All things dull and ugly'**.

Explain!

Well, he must be the one who made dinosaurs, lions, tigers, bears, wolves, killer whales, sharks, eagles, hawks, vultures, vampire bats, pythons, rattlesnakes, rats, mice, flies, cockroaches, mosquitos, fleas, lice, tapeworms, hookworms and all those other life forms that cause either us or other animals so much pain.

He must also be responsible for earthquakes, volcanoes, droughts, famines, hurricanes, whirlwinds, fires, floods, germs, viruses and for all those physical defects such as blindness, deafness, cerebral palsy, spina bifida and insanity.

And finally he must also take the blame for all the **'dull and ugly things'** that come from human beings - things like hate, greed, selfishness, lies, cruelty, violence and wars.

So should we really be singing hymns of thanks to God? Wouldn't it make more sense to protest and complain? Surely if God is **'All powerful'** and **'All good'** then he could have made a better universe than the one we've got?

1 What things do you like about our universe?

2 How would you improve on the universe we've got?

3 If you were a cockroach would your answer to number one and two change? Give details.

4 Do you think that this world would be a better place if human beings were not here? Give reasons for your answer.

RESEARCH

A Read Psalm 9 and try to sum up this writer's attitude to the universe and to human beings in particular.

I BLAME THE DEVIL

Well I believe that when God first made the world there were no earthquakes, volcanoes, droughts, famines, violence, illnesses, deformities or death. The world was just like a beautiful garden in which all human beings and other animals lived in perfect harmony with each other because they obeyed God's laws. However, a wicked spiritual power called the **devil** persuaded the first man and woman to disobey these laws. He told them that they didn't need God looking after them, that life would be better without his laws and that they should do whatever they wanted to do.

And because they obeyed the devil and disobeyed God, evil was let loose into the world and has changed it from a peaceful garden into a battlefield where God and the devil are fighting for control using us as their soldiers. So don't blame God for all the things that go wrong with our world. If human beings hadn't obeyed the devil the world would not be such a **devilish** place.

1 This explanation for evil comes from a story in Genesis chapter 3. Read this story and explain in detail:

(a) How human beings were persuaded to let evil into the world.

(b) The consequences of obeying evil (Genesis 3:14-20).

2 Do you think we can get God off the hook by blaming the devil for all the pain in the world? Give reasons for your answer.

COVERING UP FOR GOD

Well I think you're just covering up for God by trying to pin the blame for evil on the devil and human beings. . . and I don't think your cover story works.

Well, for a start there is no evidence from science that there was ever a time in our world when there weren't things like earthquakes or when animals lived in harmony with each other. In fact, archaeology tells us that the forces of nature have always been violent and animals have always been tearing each other to pieces, even before the arrival of human beings on this earth. So to say that these things started to happen after the first humans obeyed an evil power called the devil just doesn't fit the facts.

And in any case the whole idea of an evil power called the devil, declaring war on God and his world is totally nonsense because:

(1) If God is the **CREATOR** of all things then he must have created the devil.

(2) If God is **ALL-KNOWING** then he must have known in advance that the devil would turn out to be his enemy.

(3) And if God is **ALL-POWERFUL** then he could crush the devil any time he wants.

So your alibi for God doesn't get him off the hook. As far as I can see he's the brains behind the universe and he alone should take responsibility for everything that is going on in it.

1 The boy in this chapter says that you can't cover up for God by simply blaming the devil. Do you agree with his reasons for saying this? Give reasons for your answer.

2 When film makers want to portray the powers of **'good'** and **'evil'** they often do so through mythological creatures like Superman and Dracula. Make a list of these different creatures and try to explain what each creature is saying about the power of **'good'** and **'evil.'**

3 Many people say that the story in Genesis 3 actually did not take place in history. Instead, they say it is a Mythological story trying to explain truths about the powers of **'good'** and **'evil.'** They say, for example, that the 'garden' in the story is the human mind. If this is true try to explain the meaning of the story (you will need to read it again and analyse it in detail).

4 Many people say that inside all human beings there is a battle going on between good and evil. If you agree, either write your own mythological story or draw a picture to illustrate the battle going on inside you. Try to be as imaginative as film makers without using their ideas.

RESEARCH

A Find out what a scientist called Charles Darwin said about life on this earth at the beginning of time and explain why he would have said that Genesis is not history but a mythological story.

I BLAME THE WICKED

If people don't get punished occasionally then they end up getting away with murder and that's why good parents, teachers, police officers and judges make sure that those 'who try it on' experience some sort of pain to fit their crime. Of course they don't enjoy this part of their job, but they understand that for the sake of the majority, crime must go hand in hand with punishment. Otherwise, law and order will break down and that will lead to total chaos.

Now God is like a parent, a teacher, a police officer and a judge all rolled into one and his job is to maintain **law and order** in the universe. This means that occasionally he has to punish people who break his laws. He doesn't enjoy this part of his job either because he is a God of love, but he also understands that for the sake of the majority the bad people must experience some sort of pain.

This pain will always vary to fit the crime (because he is a God of justice).

For minor offences it will involve things like missing a penalty during an important match, failing an exam, a boil on your neck, an ingrown toenail, piles, treading in things deposited on pavements by dogs, pigeons depositing similar things on your head, measles, mumps.

More serious crimes will involve things like breaking a leg, heavy objects falling on you from tall ladders, a car hitting you while crossing a road, losing your boyfriend or girlfriend to someone else, baldness.

And very serious crimes will be dealt with by lightening, earthquakes, famines, droughts and deadly diseases.

1. What is the most physically or mentally painful thing that has happened to you? Illustrate your answer.
2. Do you think that the pain you experienced was a punishment from God? Give reasons for your answer.
3. Do you ever feel that you deserve to be punished by God and that it is only a matter of time before he gets you? Give reasons for your answer.

So as far as I'm concerned, God doesn't need to apologise for the pain in this world. Pain is God's way of punishing the wicked. Without it **'law and order'** would disappear, the bad would take over and this world would be more painful than it is at the moment.

YOUR GOD IS A PSYCHOPATH

This sort of explanation for pain in the world is just as nonsensical as the one that tried to put the blame on the devil.

WHAT'S WRONG WITH IT?

Well are you seriously trying to say that when people die in earthquakes, hurricanes, famines and droughts that God always selects the worst behaved people to be killed? Are you also saying that when very young children die in these calamities or of deadly diseases that they are being punished for their sins?

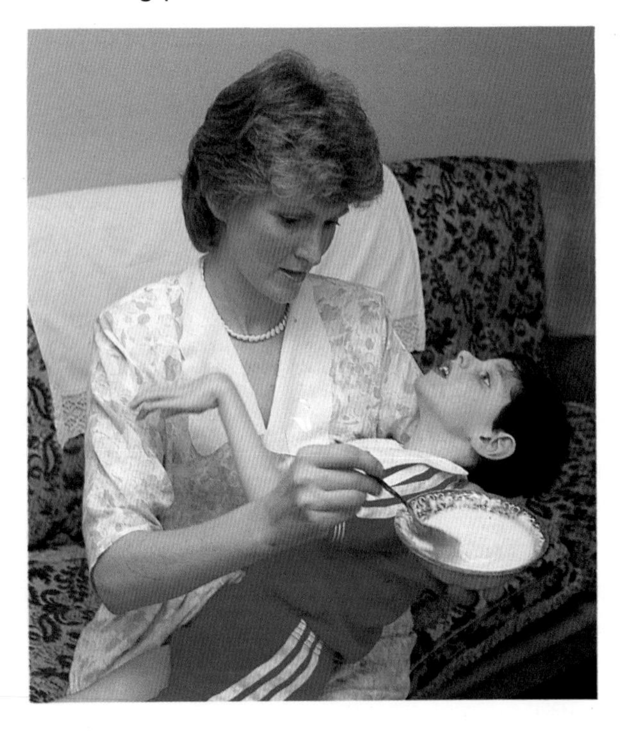

And how would you explain babies who are born blind or deaf, or with mental problems? Did they commit crimes inside their mother before they were born? In any case what sorts of crimes deserve such punishments? No good parent, teacher, police officer or judge would torture people in this way no matter what their crime, so why should a **'good God'** select people for this sort of pain? It seems to me that the kind of God you believe in behaves just like a **psychopath.**

Hundreds die at Mecca

During this year's pilgrimage to Mecca in Saudi Arabia, hundreds of Muslims were killed when crowds performing a ritual to stone the devil suddenly panicked and stampeded.

Childminder strangles charges

5 young children were strangled by a 15 year old girl from the Sudan who told police that Jesus had instructed her to end their lives.

Missionary family dies in Airbus crash

A young missionary couple asked the members of their church to pray that they would have a safe journey to their new posting in Nepal. However, the plane crashed killing them and their three young children.

Rebels slay 13 priests

13 clergymen have been shot and killed by rebels in Rwanda. This follows a previous massacre in which 9 priests and 63 civilians were killed in the country's capital.

Monk 18th victim of Spain's forest fires

An elderly monk, trapped yesterday by flames encircling his monastery, was burned alive. One horrified monk said, 'I saw how his habit caught fire, but there was nothing I could do to help him.'

Innocent student killed in drugs deal

Yesterday two robbers were given life sentences for shooting dead an innocent young student they thought was a local drug dealer. A parent of the student said, 'We both believe in God but we find it difficult to understand why he allowed our son to be killed because he was such a good person.'

Christian woman pleads for mercy

A young woman pleaded with her attacker that she was a committed Christian but was told: 'pray to Jesus to save you'. The man proceeded to bludgeon her to a point beyond recognition.

1 Look at the newspaper articles on this page. Do you think that these are examples of God punishing the wicked? Give reasons for your answers.

2 The boy in this chapter wouldn't believe they are. Explain why not.

3 Do you agree with him? Give reasons.

RESEARCH

A Did Jesus believe that when you experience 'pain' you are being punished by God? Read the following passages before writing your answer:

Luke 7:21

Luke 8:26-39

Luke 9:51-55

John 9:1-3.

B Hindus believe that we experience 'pain' because of the 'law of karma'. Find out about this 'law' and explain what it is.

C Invite a Muslim to your school to explain whether they believe that God punishes the wicked on this earth by giving them a painful experience.

FREEDOM IS PAINFUL

If you want to understand why there is pain in the world you must first of all understand that when God made human beings he didn't want a creature that would behave like a puppet on a string, always doing what he wanted because they had no choice in the matter.

Instead, he wanted to create a creature that had the power **TO CHOOSE** how it wanted to behave. In other words, a creature that was **FREE** to be bad or good.

Unfortunately, human beings often choose to behave badly and it is this choice that causes so much pain in the world. So don't blame God for hate, violence and wars. These 'pains' have been caused by human beings misusing God's gift of **FREE WILL.**

BUT THIS ONLY EXPLAINS SOME OF THE PAINS IN OUR WORLD. WHAT ABOUT EARTHQUAKES, VOLCANOS, DROUGHTS AND DISEASE? THEY'VE GOT NOTHING TO DO WITH OUR FREE WILL.

It's true that our free will didn't **cause** these PAINS but without these sorts of things being possible I don't think we would actually be free because in order to be able **'to choose'** you must have a **real choice** between alternatives and without 'pain' existing in the world this **real choice** wouldn't exist. Imagine for example, a world where there was no sort of pain.

In this world you could either greet your teacher with a smile or slap him or her round the face.

Drive your bike on the road or drive it off a cliff.

Have a party in a house or in a sewer.

In each case making a choice would be a total waste of time because no choice would cause any sort of harm. . . In other words, we might as well be puppets on a string.

So you see that these 'pains' also have something to do with our free will because without them we wouldn't have any **REAL CHOICES** and without **REAL CHOICES** we wouldn't actually be free. God therefore had to make a world where pain is possible because without pain there can be no freedom. . . and so no human beings.

1 The girl in this chapter believes that much of the 'pain' in this world is caused by our free will. Explain.

2 She also believes that things like earthquakes, volcanoes, droughts and diseases are necessary in this world if we are to be free. Explain.

3 Do you think that it is possible for us to be free in a world without 'pain'? Give reasons for your answer.

4 Do you think that this argument explains why animals experience so much suffering?

IS FREEDOM WORTH ALL THE PAIN?

Well at least your explanation for 'pain' in the world is more thoughtful than the previous two. However, I have two things to say:

First of all, imagine living in a universe where the only colour is blue. Now when it came to deciding on the colour scheme of your bedroom you wouldn't have any **REAL CHOICES** because you would be totally unaware of other colours. However, all it would take to give you a **real choice** would be for this universe to have **tiny spots** of other colours within it.

Now you say that in a universe without 'pain' I wouldn't have any **REAL CHOICES** to make but surely all it would take to give me a **real choice** would be for this universe to contain **tiny spots** of 'pain' . . . My question then is, why did God go over the top and splash so much 'pain' around the universe? Surely he could have given us freedom and a much easier life by using it more sparingly?

And secondly even if all this 'pain' in the universe is necessary for human beings to be free, is our freedom really that important? Is it worth the price? Before you answer let's look at two examples of children suffering, in a book by a Russian writer called Dostoevsky:

It so happened that one day an eight year old boy, playing in the courtyard, threw a stone and inadvertently hit the general's favourite hound in the leg, injuring it. 'Why is my favourite hound limping?' the general demanded, and he was informed that the boy had hit her with a stone. 'So it was you,' the general said, looking at the boy up and down. 'Lock him up.' They took the boy away from his mother and locked him up in the guardroom for the whole night. The next day, at dawn, the general rode out to the hunt in full dress, surrounded by his obsequious neighbours, hounds, kennel attendants, huntsmen, everyone of them on horseback. All the serfs of the estate were summoned too, for their edification, and so was the boy's mother. They brought the boy out of the guardroom. It was a bleak, foggy, raw day - an ideal day for hunting. The general ordered the boy stripped naked. The boy was shivering. He seemed paralysed with fear. He didn't dare utter a sound. 'Off with him now, chase him! ' 'Hey, you, run, run!' A flunkey yelled, and the boy started to run. 'Sic 'im!' the general roared. The whole pack was set on the boy and the hounds tore him to pieces before his mother's eyes.

And so these parents subjected their five-year-old girl to all kinds of torture. They beat her, kicked her, flogged her, for no reason that they themselves knew of. The child's whole body was covered with bruises. Eventually they devised a new refinement. Under the pretext that the child dirtied her bed they forced her to eat excrement, smearing it all over her face. And it was the mother who did it! And then that woman would lock her little daughter up in the outhouse until morning and she did so even on the coldest nights, when it was freezing. Just imagine the woman being able to sleep with the child's cries coming from that infamous outhouse. Imagine the little creature unable even to understand what is happening to her, ... weeping hot, unresentful tears, and begging 'gentle Jesus' to help her, and all this happening in that icy, dark, stinking place! ... Tell me, do you understand the purpose of that absurdity? Who needs it and why was it created? They say that man could not do without it on earth, for otherwise he would not be able to learn the difference between good and evil. But I say I'd rather not know about their damned good and evil than pay such a terrible price for it. I feel that all universal knowledge is not worth that child's tears ...

And I agree with this writer because if this is the price of freedom then I think I'd rather not have it.

1 The boy in this chapter believes that our freedom could exist with less 'pain' in the universe. Explain his point of view.

2 If you could remove three sorts of 'pain' from this world what would they be? Give reasons for your choice.

3 The boy is also not sure that our 'freedom' is worth all the pain in our world. What do you think? Perhaps you could answer this question by writing down a list of all the good that comes from being 'free' and all the bad (don't forget to come to a conclusion after the lists have been made).

4 Draw a picture or write a poem to express the 'pain' that others can't see but which you experience inside yourself. (Remember that 'pain' includes things like depression, fear, worry, anxiety, boredom.) Try to be imaginative in the way you express this pain i.e. don't just draw a sad face. Instead think of shapes, colours or even animals that might express your suffering.

PAIN CAN BE MEANINGFUL?

Many religious people will tell you that religion cannot **EXPLAIN** why an all powerful and good God allows so much suffering in the world. They say that while we are on this earth it will always remain a mystery. However, they do say that religion can help you to face suffering without despair by offering you a **MEANING** to your pain.

Well they often compare life on this earth to a journey along a road that is full of painful obstacles. These obstacles appear to have no purpose apart from making our journey uncomfortable and dangerous and when we face them we are often tempted to think that the obstacles are not worth tackling, that the road is probably going nowhere special and that the journey (and overcoming the obstacles) therefore has no purpose.

However, religion tells us that the obstacles are worth tackling. It cannot explain why the obstacles are there or why they cause us so much pain when we try to overcome them. However, it does say that the road is going somewhere special and that when we arrive and meet God after death, we will be able to look back and see the **meaning** and **purpose** of all the pain we had to endure during the journey.

Christians will often use the life of Jesus as an example of what they mean. This man, they say, had to face many obstacles during his journey in this world. He was abandoned by his family and friends, ridiculed, betrayed by a close companion, arrested, beaten, tortured and eventually nailed to a cross to endure a slow and agonising death.

And at various times in his life he, like us, was tempted to think that the pain involved was senseless. However, Jesus was a man whose trust in God was stronger than his doubts. He chose to believe that his suffering, although it often appeared senseless, nevertheless had **MEANING** and it was this choice to accept whatever happened as God's will that gave him the courage to continue his journey to the end.

Jesus then chose to believe that God gave his painful life meaning (even though he did not fully understand it himself) and that, say religious people is the choice we all have, for whether we like it or not we are all on the journey of life and when we meet our obstacles we, like Jesus, must also decide whether they are **meaningful** or **meaningless.**

A writer called Fitz James Stephen sums up this choice in the following way:

> *What do you think of yourself? What do you think of the world? ... These are questions with which all must deal as it seems good to them. They are riddles of the sphinx, and in some way or other we must deal with them ... in all important transactions of life we have to take a leap in the dark ... If we decide to leave the riddles unanswered, that is a choice; if we waver in our answer, that, too, is a choice: but whatever choice we make, we make it at our peril. If a man chooses to turn his back altogether on God and the future, no one can prevent him; no one can show beyond reasonable doubt that he is mistaken. If a man thinks otherwise and acts as he thinks, I do not see that anyone can prove that he is mistaken. Each must act as he thinks best; and if he is wrong, so much the worst for him. We stand on a mountain pass in the midst of whirling snow and blinding mist, through which we get glimpses now and then of paths which may be deceptive. If we stand still we shall be frozen to death. If we take the wrong road we shall be dashed to pieces. We do not certainly know whether there is any right one. What must we do? 'Be strong and of a good courage.' Act for the best, hope for the best, and take what comes ... If death ends all, we cannot meet death better.*

1 What is life compared to in this chapter? Do you agree? Give reasons.

2 This chapter also says that religion doesn't explain suffering. Instead it offers us meaning. Explain.

3 Do you think that there may be some meaning to suffering and that after death we will understand its purpose fully? Give reasons for your answer.

RESEARCH

A Many religious people (like Jesus) were tempted to think that life is meaningless. Read the following passages and in each case explain what happened:

(1) 1 Kings 19

(2) Psalm 22

(3) Luke 22:39-45

(4) Matthew 27:26-50.

B Find out about the life of one of the following religious people and try to work out which of their painful experiences may have tempted them or others to think that life has no meaning:

(1) The prophet Mohammed

(2) Gandhi

(3) Guru Nanak

(4) Desmond Tutu.

C Have you ever had an experience that has made you think that life is either meaningful or meaningless? Give details.

IF I WERE GOD I'D SACK MYSELF

1 Have you, like this monk, ever made a request to God and the outcome was the complete opposite of what you wanted? Try to think of an example and write it down.

2 Why do you think these sorts of things happen?

PRAYERS ARE LIKE SPELLS

If you want to know why some prayers don't get answered then you must first of all understand that God is a power that we can tap into if we know the right code to use. Prayers, then, are just like **spells.** Know the right magical code to use and this power will help you out. Get the code wrong and your prayers will not be answered.

WHAT CODE ARE YOU TALKING ABOUT?

Well there isn't just one magical code that you can use. Like spells, there can be different types. Sometimes, for example, the code will involve reciting long prayers, chanting special holy words, making sacred movements with your hands, sitting in a particular way, burning incense, lighting candles, spinning wheels, moving and counting beads on a thread or making some personal sacrifice that might involve you suffering in some way.

So you have a choice. However, make sure that you get your chosen code (like a spell) exactly right. One detail wrong is all it takes for you not to gain access to this power and for your prayers not to be answered.

1. Many people behave as if there is a power in the universe that you can keep on your good side by performing 'magical' rituals e.g. throwing salt over your shoulder when you spill it or touching the colour black. Try to think of other examples of things people do in order to get favours from this power.
2. Do you sometimes perform a ritual in order to get good luck?
3. Do you think these rituals work?

RESEARCH

A. Not all people who burn incense, light candles, chant special words, spin wheels, etc. do so in order to get something from God. Invite a priest to your school and ask him why these rituals are performed in many places of worship (you could of course research this answer yourself).

B. What do you think Jesus would have said about magical rituals that try to get something from God? Read Matthew 6:7-8.

BRIBE GOD TO GET AN ANSWER

I also believe that God is a power, but not the sort of impersonal magical power that you can use by reciting a code. This power is more like a parent who gives you what you want when you're in their good books and ignores what you want when you're not. In other words, God will give you what you want when you deserve it, just like a parent.

So before you approach God with a request, get on his good side by being good. Keep your head down, stay out of trouble, and do as you're told. Be nice, and God is more likely to be nice to you by listening to what you've got to say and answering your prayer.

Of course, if you're a bit of a devil you've got problems. But all is not lost. What you need to do (as with a parent) is to worm your way into his good books by promising to be extra good in the future. Promise, for example, never to doubt his existence again, to say your prayers regularly, to be kind to your brother or sister - even to go to church, synagogue or temple occasionally. In this way God might be persuaded to give you what you want on credit. However, you must do a good job in convincing him that you will be able to pay him back – don't make promises that you don't intend to keep.

1 When you want something from your parents it generally helps to be on their good side. What do you do in order to convince your parents that you deserve whatever you want from them?

2 If God exists how do you think we could get on his good side?

3 Have you ever tried to do a deal with God by making promises of future good behaviour in order to obtain a few favours? Give details of the deal and the outcome.

YOU DON'T HAVE ENOUGH TRUST

Unanswered prayer has nothing to do with not being in God's good books. It has more to do with a lack of trust. In other words, your prayers don't get answered because you don't really believe that there is a God, or if you do, you don't really believe that he can help you. Those who have learnt to trust God completely get answers to prayers.

Many vicars, for example, will tell you of occasions when they have prayed for money to repair a church roof and of this money miraculously arriving in the nick of time. Many believers will have stories of praying for sick people and of these people being cured of their illnesses. And others will tell you of situations where they were in danger of losing their lives and of God answering their prayers by rescuing them.

1 Conduct a survey amongst your family and friends and try to find at least six people who claim to have had an answer to prayer. Then ask them the following questions and write down their replies:

(a) What was your answer to prayer?

(b) Why do you think God answered your prayer?

(c) Why do you think God answered your prayer and not the prayers of many in the world who are dying of hunger and disease?

2 Do you think that the people in your survey had real answers to prayer? Give reasons for your answer.

GOD ALWAYS ANSWERS PRAYERS

I believe that God answers everybody's prayers whether their faith is strong or weak. He never ignores anybody who comes to him with a request. However, his answer is not always **'Yes'**.

Sometimes the answer to your prayer will have to be **'No'** because God, like a good parent, will only give you things that are good for you. If you request something that will harm you God's response will have to be negative.

On other occasions God's answer may be **'Yes . . . but not yet'**, because God, like a good parent, will only give you what you want when you are ready for it. If then you request something that is unsuitable for you at the moment then God's response will be **'Wait'**.

And finally, God's response to your prayer may be to give you something that you never even requested because God, once again like a good parent, knows your needs better than you know them yourself. God's answer to your prayer will therefore often be different to the answer you wanted but it will always be better . . . **because God knows best**.

1. We often think we will be happy if we possess certain things. Make a list of the things which you wanted when you were much younger. Do you still think that having these things will make you happy? Give reasons.
2. Make a list of the things you want now. Do you think that in another ten years time you will look back on these 'wants' and wonder how you ever thought that they could make you happy?
3. Try to remember occasions when you have been very angry with your parents because they said 'No' to something you wanted and which you now realise was the best answer.
4. The boy on this page believes that God always answers our prayers. Explain his point of view.
5. Can you think of anything wrong with his ideas?

GOD CAN'T COPE

What you have said about God has totally confused me

Well, if what you say about God is true, then he's nothing like my idea of a good parent. In fact, he comes across as the sort of parent who doesn't have a clue about looking after a large family.

Why, for example, does God say **'Yes'** to those of his children who want money for a new church roof or a cure to their cancer and **'No'** to the millions of his children throughout the world who don't even have a roof over their heads and who are dying of poverty and disease?

Why does he also say **'Yes'** to small numbers of his children who need rescuing from dangerous situations and **'No'** to children like the six million Jews who died in Nazi gas chambers. **Does this mean that God has favourites?**

Why, for example, should I bother to ask God for anything if God always knows what's best for me? If, as you say, God is like a parent who knows what I need better than I know myself, wouldn't it be easier to simply wait for what he is going to do and then lump it? If my requests are only going to get a 'Yes' when they agree with what he wants, then surely there's no point in making requests.

And in any case, if God is a good parent, then I shouldn't need to ask him for help. If he is going to do his job properly, then like any good parent, he should be helping me with my problems whether I ask him to or not.

1. The boy in this chapter thinks there is a lot wrong with the previous ideas about prayer. Explain why he thinks this in your own words.
2. Do you agree? Give reasons for your answer.

RESEARCH

A. Invite a religious leader to your class and ask him/her to reply to the ideas expressed in this chapter.

YOU CAN'T CHANGE GOD'S MIND

Many religious people would say that the reason why so many are confused about PRAYER is that they haven't understood the difference between **talking to God** and **talking to a human being** (like a parent). God, they say, may often be described as a human being (to help us understand the way he behaves towards us) but he isn't one, so talking to him will be very different to having a chat with your Mum or Dad.

Well there are of course many but perhaps the most important one for our understanding of prayer is that **when you talk to a human being, you are talking to a being that doesn't know everything.** This means that in your conversation you can give them information that they didn't already know and by so doing occasionally change their minds.

However, **when you talk to God you are talking to a being who knows everything.** This means that when you talk to God you can't give him any information that he didn't already know and so consequently you can't change his mind about anything.

WELL IF GOD KNOWS EVERYTHING AND HE'S NEVER GOING TO CHANGE HIS MIND ABOUT ANYTHING, WHY BOTHER TALKING TO HIM? ISN'T MAKING REQUESTS TO GOD MEANINGLESS?

Well, if you think that the purpose of prayer is to twist God's arm, change his mind and make him do what you want, then talking to God does seem a waste of time. However, according to many religious people that isn't the purpose of prayer. Instead, they say that **prayer is not an opportunity to change God's mind but to change the mind of the person who is praying.** The following prayer may help to explain what they mean:

FOR A LONG TIME, LORD I THOUGHT THAT TO BE FREE MEANT THAT I COULD DO JUST ABOUT ANYTHING. ANYTHING THAT OCCURRED TO ME OR THAT I FELT LIKE DOING – THE WILDEST THINGS.

I NOW KNOW, LORD, WHAT IT MEANS TO BE FREE. IT MEANS TO DESIRE WHAT YOU DESIRE, TO LOVE WHAT YOU LOVE. AND IF THERE HAS TO BE A CHOICE, IT SIMPLY MEANS THAT I TAKE WHAT YOU CHOOSE.

TO BE FREE MEANS TO TRY TO FIND OUT YOUR PURPOSE FOR MY LIFE, YOUR PLANS, AND YOUR OPINIONS, AND TO MAKE MY OWN FACE MORE LIKE YOURS.

Prayer then for many religious people is not about God coming to know anything. Instead it is seen as an opportunity for the person praying to know more about themselves (for we reveal what we are to ourselves in what we say to God), to know more about God's will for their lives and to acquire the courage to accept it.

This doesn't mean that people don't tell God what they want. However, when they do so, they are not trying to persuade God to change his mind and do them a few favours. Instead they are sharing with God their deepest desires in order that they will be changed to desire the will of God. And when this change takes place (say religious people) you will begin to understand how powerful prayer really is, for when God's will is allowed to work through you, all things are possible. . . including miracles.

Prayer then isn't seen as an opportunity to get what you want from God. Instead it is a time when **you fight for freedom from what you want.** That's why many religious people will always end their requests to God with the words 'THY WILL BE DONE'.

1. This chapter says that there are important differences between talking to a human being and talking to God. In your own words explain the difference discussed in this chapter. Can you think of any other differences?
2. This chapter also says that because there is this difference the purpose of prayer cannot be 'to change the mind of God.' What then (according to this chapter) is the purpose of prayer?
3. **'Prayer is a time when you often fight for freedom from what you want.'** What do you think this means? (Look at the prayer on page 33 to help you with the answer.)
4. Do you agree? Give reasons for your answer.

RESEARCH

A Do you think that Jesus would have agreed that prayer is a time when you often 'fight for freedom from what you want'? Read Luke 22:39-45. Give reasons for your answer.

B Do you think a Muslim would agree? Find out what the word 'Islam' means before giving your answer.

C Religious people will tell you that learning to accept 'God's will' doesn't mean that you simply sit back and accept whatever is happening. They say that accepting 'God's will' often means that you will have to get off your backside and do something either for yourself or other people. Read Matthew 25:31-46 and then explain what accepting 'God's will' might involve.

IF I WERE GOD I'D SEE A PSYCHIATRIST

1 If God exists and he is all good, all loving and just, do you think he would build a hellish torture chamber for the wicked to roast in for eternity? Give reasons for your answer.

GO TO HELL

Many of our ideas about hell being a torture chamber come from a book written in the fourteenth century by a man called Dante. The book is called *The Inferno* and begins with Dante in a dark wood, meeting a character called Virgil who offers to give him a guided tour of the nine pits of hell. The tour begins at the 'Gate of Hell' which has written above it the inscription: **'Abandon hope all ye who enter here'.**

In the first pit called 'Limbo' Dante meets the souls of babies who died before they were baptised and the souls of good people who died before the coming of Jesus. Dante discovers that these souls are not tortured but spend their time in green meadows enjoying the pleasures of the countryside. However, they are cut off from the far greater pleasures of heaven which are so wonderful that they are beyond expression.

Virgil then leads Dante to **the second pit** which is filled with those who spent all of their lives chasing people of the opposite sex. These people, whose lives were controlled completely by their wild passions, must now live in the middle of an everlasting storm, continually thrown about within tortuous whirlwinds.

In the third pit Dante is shown the souls of those who spent their time on the earth simply eating and drinking. These gluttons, Dante discovers, are continually having their skin ripped from their bodies by a hideous three-headed creature called Cerberus.

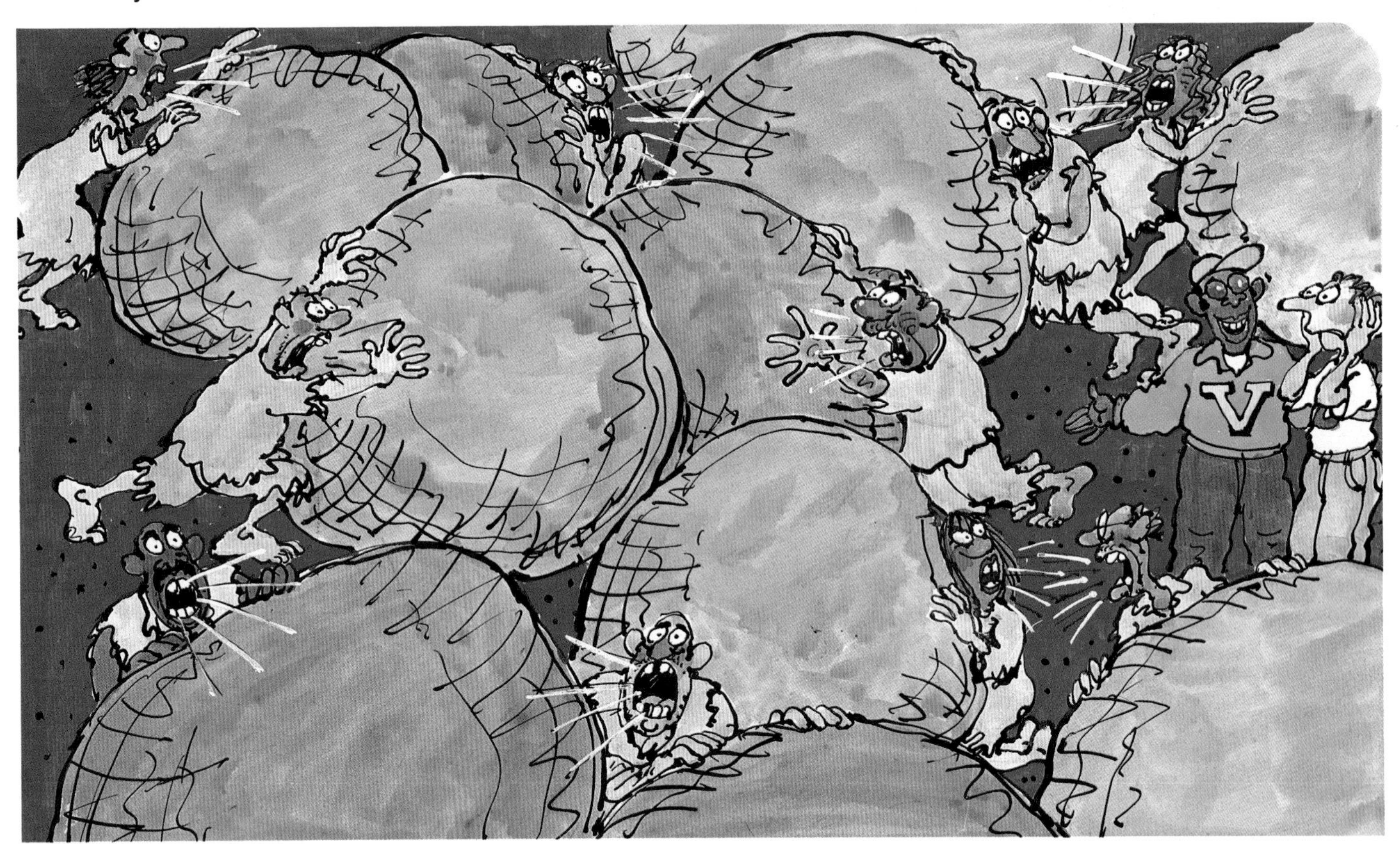

As Dante descends to **the fourth pit** he sees people pushing enormous boulders aimlessly around. They are forever getting in each other's way and spend their time swearing and cursing each other. This torture, he is told, is reserved for misers and for those fools who parted with their money too easily.

The fifth pit contains a slimy, stinking river called the Styx and immersed in its mud and filthy water are those who spent their lives being angry and sullen. These naked souls are forever covered in excrement and spend eternity fighting each other with their fists and teeth.

The sixth pit is filled with people who refused to believe the teachings of the church and who in various ways tried to change them. These **heretics** are packed together and roasted in ovens.

The seventh pit is reserved for those who were violent in their lives. These souls are forever drowning in a river of boiling blood.

Dante discovers that **the eighth pit** is subdivided into ten layers with each layer specialising in the punishment of a particular sin. Thieves, for example, spend eternity in a snake pit, liars are covered in itchy sores and those who spent their time on the earth flattering people who could be of service to them are held upside down in human excrement.

The ninth and lowest pit of all is a chamber covered in ice and is the punishment for those who betrayed others. These souls are forever frozen solid in the iced lake of Cocytus. The devil is also in this pit. He himself is frozen in ice up to his chest and is forever eating the bodies of **Judas Iscariot, Brutus and Cassius**.

1. Which pit do you think is the most horrific? Explain why.
2. If Dante's picture of hell were true into which pit do you think you might find yourself? Give reasons for your answer.
3. Think of five famous or infamous people and explain in which pit you think they might find themselves. Once again give reasons for your answer.
4. When Dante was thinking of tortures for his hell he used the tortures that were common in the fourteenth century. If you were asked to think of tortures for a hell with nine pits which would you borrow from the twentieth century? (Think of mental tortures instead of physical ones, like watching the Arsenal for eternity trying to score a goal away from home.) Illustrate your answer.

RESEARCH

A In the ninth and lowest pit of hell Satan is eating the bodies of Judas, Brutus and Cassius. Find out who they betrayed.

B When Jesus was describing hell he used the word Gehenna. Find out what this word means and try to work out what he was trying to say about hell.

DEMOLISHING DANTE'S HELL

If you think that hell is like the one described by Dante then you've got problems because in order to believe in it you will also have to believe in the geography of the fourteenth century.

Well at the time of Dante they believed that the earth was at the centre of the universe and that around the earth revolved nine spheres on which were attached the different planets and stars i.e. one for the sun, one for the moon, one for each of the five planets then known, one for the stars and one for God.

Now, they believed that one day there was a heavenly argument between God and one of his angels called Lucifer. Not being God, Lucifer, of course lost the fight and was thrown out of heaven. He fell towards earth at such a great speed that when he hit the earth somewhere near the south pole he created an enormous nine-layered pit (the one described by Dante). The dirt that came spilling out of this pit made a huge mountain called the Mountain of Purgatory from which flowed three streams. Christopher Columbus believed in this sort of geography and fully expected to come across this pit on his journeys. When in fact he turned his ship north and started sailing faster he believed it was because he was travelling downwards and away from the Mountain of Purgatory.

Today of course we know that the universe is nothing like this. The earth is not the centre of the universe. It is not surrounded by nine spheres on which are attached the different planets and stars and there is no nine-layered pit near the south pole or a Mountain of Purgatory. So if hell exists it will not be like Dante's torture chamber. This sort of hell might have made some sort of sense in the fourteenth century (although even then there were many who thought that a God of love would never create such terrible tortures for his children). Today however it is nonsense.

1 This chapter says that today it is impossible for thinking people to believe in Dante's picture of hell. Explain why.

2 When Christopher Columbus turned his ship northwards he started sailing faster. What was his explanation?

3 What would your explanation be?

RESEARCH

A If you were to be transported back to the fourteenth century what new information would you give them about the universe? You will probably need to research this answer in the library to get accurate and interesting information.

A DAY TRIP TO A MODERN HELL

Many religious people still believe in hell as a place where you experience tortuous pain. However, they do not believe that this place is a torture chamber put together by God and placed in the depths of the earth. Instead they say that hell is a place we choose to build ourselves and that it is built in the human mind. **The tortures of hell then take place inside our heads and we (and not God) are our own torturers.**

A book written by C.S. Lewis called *The Great Divorce* helps to make these ideas clear. This book compares hell to an enormous city which is ever expanding. A resident of this city explains why:

'The trouble is that they're so quarrelsome. As soon as anyone arrives he settles in some street. Before he's been there twenty-four hours he quarrels with his neighbour. Before the week is over he's quarrelled so badly that he decides to move. Very likely he finds the next street empty because all the people there have quarrelled with their neighbours and moved. If so he settles in. If by any chance the street is full, he goes further. But even if he stays, it makes no odds. He's sure to have another quarrel pretty soon and then he'll move on again. Finally he'll move right to the edge of the town and build a new house. You see, it's easy here. You've only got to **think** a house and there it is. That's how the town keeps on growing'.

Now this explanation takes place on a bus which is taking a group of residents from hell on a sight-seeing trip to heaven. When they arrive this is what happens:

'Then, suddenly we were at rest. Everyone had jumped up. Curses, taunts, blows . . . came to my ears as my fellow passengers struggled to get out. A moment later, and they all succeeded. I was alone in the bus, and through the open door there came to me in the fresh stillness the singing of a lark. I got out . . .

'At first, my attention was caught by my fellow passengers, who were still grouped about in the neighbourhood of the omnibus, though beginning, some of them, to walk forward into the landscape with hesitating steps. I gasped when I saw them. Now that they were in the light, they were transparent– fully **transparent** when they stood between me and it . . . They were in fact **ghosts**: man-shaped stains on the brightness of that air . . . I noticed that the grass did not bend under their feet: even the dew drops were not disturbed . . . It was the light, the grass, the trees that were different; made of some different substance, so much **solider** than things in our country **that men were ghosts by comparison.**'

' "I don't like it! I don't like it!" screamed a voice. "It gives me the pip!" One of the ghosts had darted past me, back into the bus. She never came out of it again as far as I know. The others remained uncertain.

' "Hi mister", said the Big Man, addressing the driver, "when have we got to go back (to hell)?" **"You need never come back unless you want to,"** he replied. "Stay (in heaven) as long as you please."

'Long after that I saw people coming to meet us. Because they were bright I saw them while they were still very distant, and at first I did not know they were people at all. Mile after mile they drew nearer. The earth shook under their tread as their feet sank into the wet turf. They came on steadily. I did not entirely like it. Two of the ghosts screamed and ran for the bus. The rest of us huddled closer to one another. As the **solid** people came nearer still I noticed that they were moving with order and determination . . . '

1. Many religious people now say that hell is not a torture chamber made by God. Where do they believe hell can be found and who do they believe has built it?
2. C.S. Lewis tried to make these ideas clear by comparing hell to a city that is ever expanding. Explain why this city is continually getting bigger.
3. When the people of hell arrived in heaven they discovered something about themselves that horrified them. Explain.
4. When C.S. Lewis described the people of hell in this way what do you think he was trying to say about them?
5. How does C.S. Lewis describe the residents of heaven? Once again try to work out what he is trying to say about them.
6. The bus driver says to a resident of hell that 'you never need come back (to hell) unless you want to. . . stay (in heaven) as long as you please'. Many wanted to go back, so what do you think C.S. Lewis is saying about these people?

RESEARCH

A. Read a short story by D.H. Lawrence called *The Man Who Loved Islands* and try to explain the connection between this story and the story in this chapter.

HELLISH AND HEAVENLY MINDS

One way of understanding this story is to think of hell and heaven as existing in our minds.

The residents of hell are therefore those people who have chosen to allow their minds to be **powered** by things like **Hate, Anger, Violence and Jealousy.** These people therefore grow further and further away from God and other people, preferring instead to be alone being **tortured** by their own selfishness. They also end up being unreal human beings who (like ghosts) have no depth to them or any real presence.

The residents of **heaven** are those who have chosen to have their minds **powered by the love of God.** These people grow nearer and nearer to God and to other people enjoying the heavenly experience of loving and being loved. They also end up being **real** and **solid** human beings with depth and real presence.

If we understand the story in this way then the writer seems to be saying a number of things about hell that are very different to what Dante said in *The Inferno.*

First of all you can be in **hell** now while you are alive on this earth because if you have the sort of mind that is totally powered by things like **hate, anger, and violence,** then you are moving further and further away from other people and that is a tortuous and hellish experience.

Secondly, hell is not created by God but by us in our own minds and it is a torture **we choose** and not one that God condemns us to have.

Thirdly, that this hellish experience of being separated from God's love and so from other people is an experience that **you can choose to have for eternity.**

C.S.Lewis sums up what he is trying to say in the following way:

There are only two kinds of people in the end: those who say to God 'Thy will be done', and those to whom God says, in the end, 'Thy will be done'. All that are in Hell choose it. Without that self-choice there could be no Hell. No soul that seriously and constantly desires joy will ever miss it. Those who seek find. To those who knock it is opened.

1 C.S. Lewis says that people in hell are those whose minds are moving further and further away from God and other people. According to this chapter how does this happen? Illustrate your answer.

2 This chapter also describes the people in hell as having **'no depth to them or any real presence.'** What do you think this means?

3 The people in heaven are described as people whose minds are moving nearer to God and other people. How does this happen? Once again illustrate your answer.

4 They are described as **'people who are solid with depth and real presence.'** What do you think this means?

5 This chapter has suggested that people who are moving further away from God and other people are in their own **self-made** hell torturing themselves and that people who are moving nearer to each other and God are in heaven. Do you agree? Perhaps your ideas could be expressed in a poem or a picture.

6 Many religious people say that you can be in **heaven** or **hell** now and that if you choose you can stay there for eternity. What do you think this means?

7 Explain some of the important differences between Dante's picture of hell and the picture given by C.S. Lewis.

8 C.S. Lewis says that 'in the end there are only two types of people.' Explain who they are and what he means.

RESEARCH

A Read Galatians 6:7-10 and Galatians 5:19-26. Try to explain what you think these passages mean and the connection between the meaning and the ideas in this chapter.

B Read a short book by Oscar Wilde called *The Portrait of Dorian Grey* and once again explain the connection between this story and the ideas in this chapter.